T0061331

If you were a

Suffix

by Marcie Aboff
illustrated by Sara Gray

PICTURE WINDOW BOOKS
Minneapolis, Minnesota

suffix a letter or group of letters added to the end of a word to change its meaning

Editor: Christianne Jones
Designer: Hilary Wacholz
Page Production: Melissa Kes
Art Director: Nathan Gassman
The illustrations in this book were created with acrylics.

Picture Window Books
1710 Roe Crest Drive
North Mankato, MN 56003
www.capstonepub.com

Copyright © 2009 by Picture Window Books, a Capstone imprint. All rights reserved. No part of this book may be reproduced without written permission from the publisher. The publisher takes no responsibility for the use of any of the materials or methods described in this book, nor for the products thereof.

Looking for suffixes?

Watch for the

Library of Congress Cataloging-in-Publication Data
Aboff, Marcie.
If you were a suffix / by Marcie Aboff ; illustrated by Sara Gray.
p. cm. — (Word fun.)
Includes index.
ISBN 978-1-4048-4774-3 (library binding)
ISBN 978-1-4048-4778-1 (paperback)
1. English language—Suffixes and prefixes—Juvenile literature.
I. Gray, Sara, ill. II. Title.
PE1175.A24 2008
428.1—dc22 2008006417

Printed in the United States 5619

Special thanks to our advisers for their expertise:

Rosemary G. Palmer, Ph.D., Department of Literacy
College of Education, Boise State University

Terry Flaherty, Ph.D., Professor of English
Minnesota State University, Mankato

... You would come last!

You could be joyful and playful!

If you were a suffix, you would be a letter or a group of letters added to the end of a word. By adding a suffix, the meaning of the word changes.

The hope<u>less</u> hippo became hope<u>ful</u> after he won the lottery.

The care<u>less</u> cat became a care<u>ful</u> cat after he used up his eighth life.

If you were the suffix "er," you would be the one who does something.

The teach<u>er</u> taught the bank<u>er</u> how to count.

Then the bank<u>er</u> taught the bak<u>er</u>,

the baker taught
the farmer,

and the
farmer
taught the
trainer.

If you were the suffix "s" or "es," you would make things plural.
The bear and fox ran toward the bush.
Other bears and foxes hid behind the bushes.

One horse jumped over a fence.
Three horses jumped over many fences.

If you were the suffix "ful," you would mean "full of."

The clumsy waiter spilled a cup<u>ful</u> of coffee all over the king.

To make matters worse, it happened in front of a roomful of people.

If you were the suffix "less," you would mean "without."

The fear<u>less</u> eagle soared
into the end<u>less</u> sky.

The careless elephant almost stepped on the harmless mouse.
The tasteless zebra thought the pretty dress was useless.

If you were the suffix "est," you would state the size of something. You would always be the extreme.

The tallest giraffe and the shortest monkey were best friends.

The biggest rhino and the smallest bird were best friends, too.

The four friends crossed over the widest river.

If you were the suffix "d" or "ed," you would change a word from present tense to past tense.

The frog likes to hop and jump.
The frog hopped on the stones
and jumped into the water.

Mama pig can oink loudly.
She oink<u>ed</u> at the piglets until
they return<u>ed</u> to the pigpen.

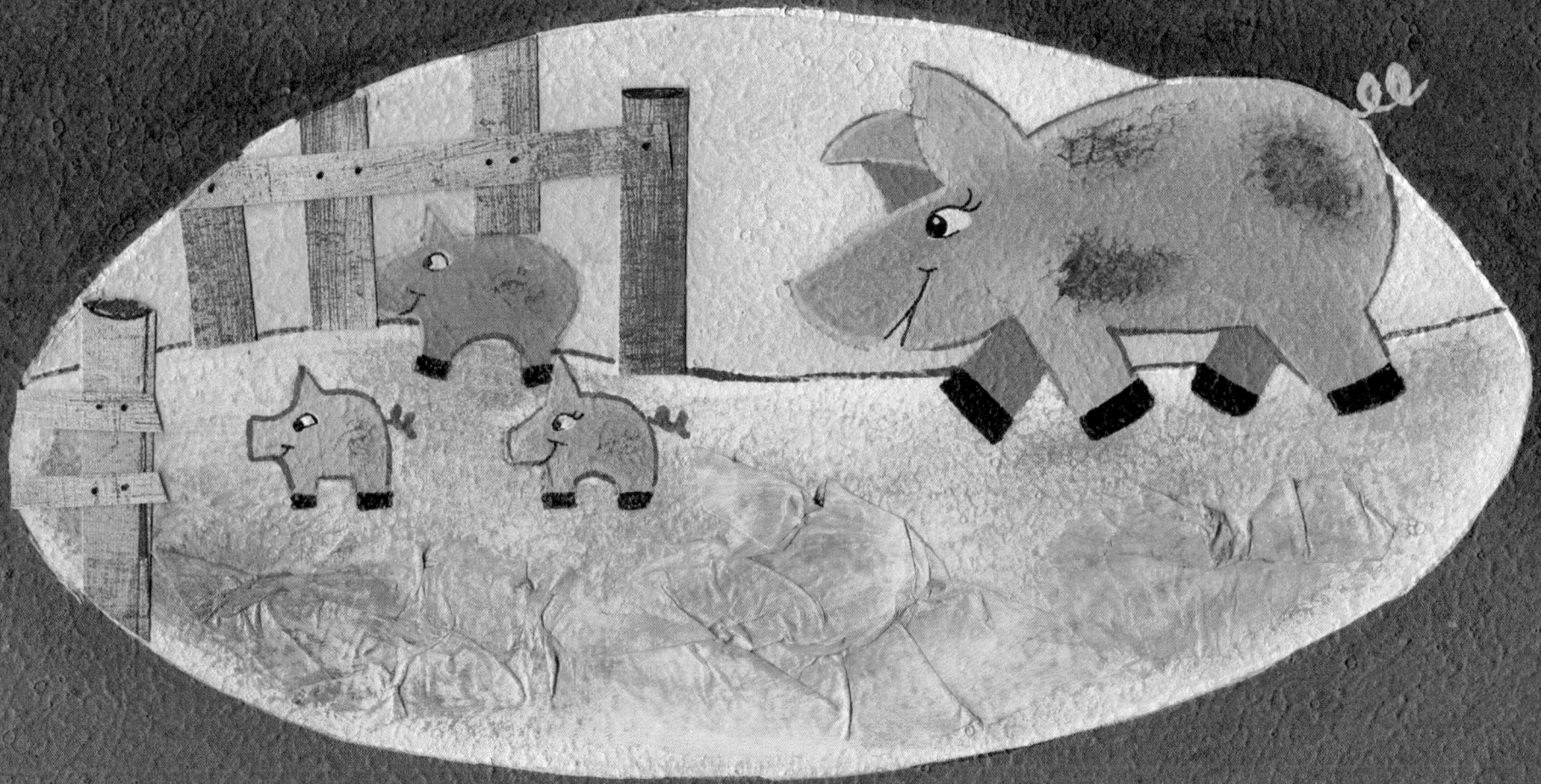

If you were a suffix, you could change the spelling of the root word.

The dogs sat by the pool.
They liked sitting by the pool.

If you were a suffix, you might drop a letter and add a new letter. The letter "y" is often replaced by the letter "i."

There were **plenty** of poppies in the field.
The poppies were **plentiful**.

Peacocks have feathers of great **beauty**.
Their feathers are **beautiful**.

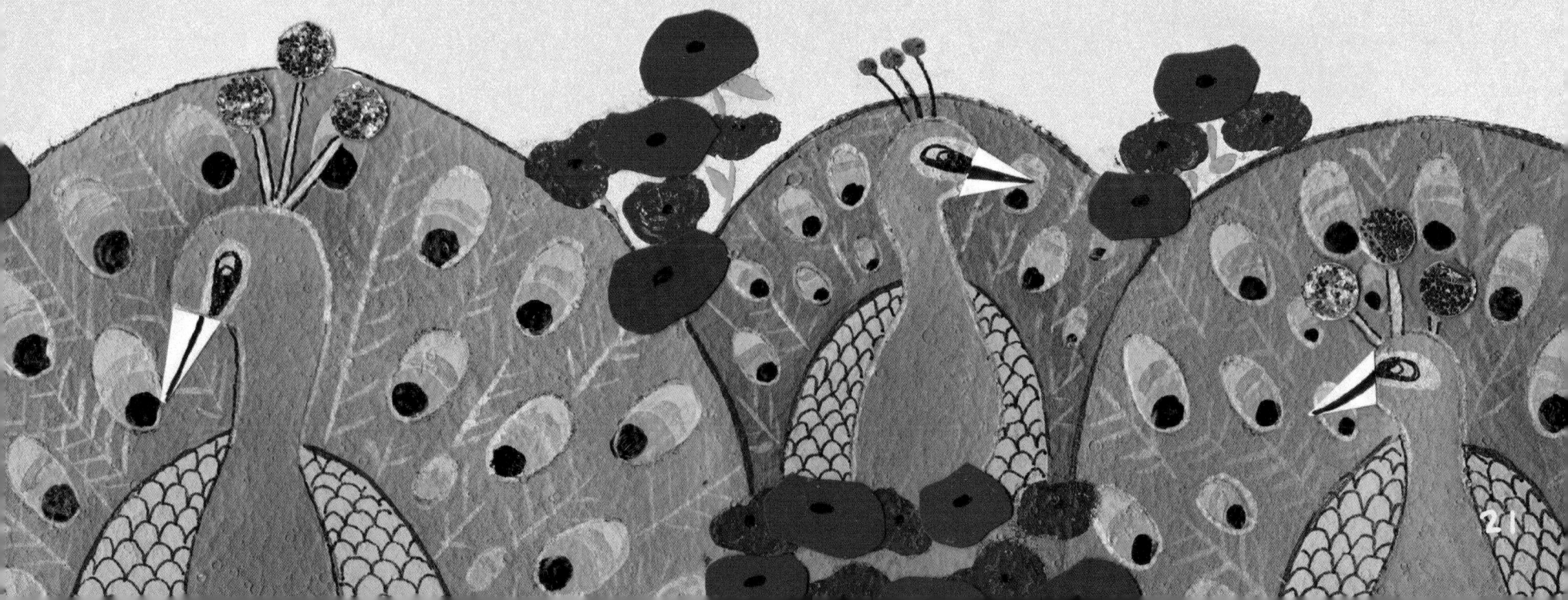

You would be the perfect ending ...
THE
END
... if you were
a suffix.

FUN WITH PREFIXES

Cut out 14 pieces of paper. On each piece of paper, write one of the prefixes or root words from below. Mix them up and see if you can put the words back together. Then make your own list and have a friend match the words. You can even time each other and see who can match the words faster.

mis place
un finished

non sense
mid way

pre view
tele cast

over work

Glossary

extraordinary—more than ordinary
multicolored—having many colors
prefix—a letter or group of letters placed before a word to change its meaning
rebounded—to gain possession of the basketball after a shot
root—the basic meaning of the word
transformed—changed form

To Learn More

More Books to Read

Draze, Dianne. *Red Hot Root Words.* Austin, Tex.: Dandy Lion Publications, 2003.

Heinrichs, Ann. *Prefixes and Suffixes.* Chanhassen, Minn.: Child's World, 2006.

Langton, Charan. *Big Words for Little Kids.* San Ramon, Calif.: Mountcastle Company, 2007.

On the Web

FactHound offers a safe, fun way to find Web sites related to topics in this book. All of the sites on FactHound have been researched by our staff.

1. Visit *www.facthound.com*
2. Type in this special code: 1404847731
3. Click on the FETCH IT button.

Your trusty FactHound will fetch the best sites for you!

Index

added meaning, 14-15
different meaning, 16-17
opposites, 18-19
prefix "co," 10-11
prefix definition, 6, 20
prefix "re," 8-9
prefix "tele," 12-13

Look for all of the books in the Word Fun series:

If You Were a Compound Word
If You Were a Conjunction
If You Were a Contraction
If You Were a Homonym or a Homophone
If You Were a Noun
If You Were a Palindrome
If You Were a Prefix
If You Were a Preposition
If You Were a Pronoun
If You Were a Suffix
If You Were a Synonym
If You Were a Verb
If You Were Alliteration
If You Were an Adjective
If You Were an Adverb
If You Were an Antonym
If You Were an Interjection
If You Were Onomatopoeia